W9-AUJ-135

GRANDMA'S SWEET TREATS

GRANDMA'S SWEET TREATS

DELICIOUS RECIPES FROM GRANDMA'S KITCHEN

This edition published in 2013
LOVE FOOD is an imprint of Parragon Books Ltd

Parragon
Chartist House
15–17 Trim Street
Bath, BA1 1HA, UK

www.parragon.com/lovefood

ISBN: 978-1-78186-809-6

Printed in China

Introduction and Grandma's tips by Linda Doeser
New recipes by Beverly LeBlanc
Edited by Fiona Biggs
Additional photography and styling by Mike Cooper
Additional home economy by Lincoln Jefferson
Internal design by Sarah Knight

Notes for the Reader
This book uses standard kitchen measuring spoons and cups. All spoon and cup measurements are level unless otherwise indicated. Unless otherwise stated, milk is assumed to be whole, eggs are large, individual vegetables are medium, and pepper is freshly ground black pepper. Unless otherwise stated, all root vegetables should be washed and peeled before using.

Garnishes and serving suggestions are all optional and not necessarily included in the recipe ingredients or method. The times given are only an approximate guide. Preparation times differ according to the techniques used by different people and the cooking times may also vary from those given. Optional ingredients, variations, or serving suggestions have not been included in the calculations.

Recipes using raw or very lightly cooked eggs should be avoided by infants, the elderly, pregnant women, and people with weakened immune systems. Pregnant and breast-feeding women are advised to avoid eating peanuts and peanut products. People with nut allergies should be aware that some of the prepared ingredients used in the recipes in this book may contain nuts. Always check the packaging before use.

Picture acknowledgments
The publisher would like to thank the following for permission to reproduce copyright material:
Stack of cups and saucers © Alexandra Grablewski/Getty images
Vintage labels © AKaiser/Shutterstock
Close-up notepaper on cork board © Picsfive/Shutterstock
A coffee cup stain © Tyler Olson/Shutterstock
Masking tape © Samantha Grandy/Shutterstock
Vintage prints supplied courtesy of Istock Images

Contents

INTRODUCTION

Grandmas know how to do things—this is because they have a wealth of experience and, over time, have discovered the best, easiest, and most efficient ways of tackling whatever tasks they've set their minds to. The only mistakes we learn from are our own, but if we're smart, we'll learn from the many things that grandmas have got right and use all their clever ways to save time, effort, and even money when preparing irresistible cakes, cookies, tarts, desserts, and other sweet treats.

This book is far more than just an inspiring collection of scrumptious recipes or a stroll through the delightful memory lanes of childhood; it is also an anthology of the accumulated kitchen wisdom of grandmas and even grandmas' grandmas. With each generation, traditional recipes have been lovingly adapted before being passed on, so now they are ideally suited to today's busy lifestyle and have been modified to make full use of modern kitchen equipment without losing that special home-baked quality.

Nothing makes us feel so cherished or offers so much cozy comfort as freshly home-baked delights, whether a light-as-air snack-time cake, a fabulous fruit pie for dessert, a satisfying baked pudding, or decadent special-occasion treats. All the recipes in this book are easy to follow, calling for little more than good old-fashioned common sense and, perhaps, a pinch of care and affection.

The recipes are divided into four chapters, each filled with traditional sweet treats to suit every occasion. Grandma's Family Favorites includes all the much-loved snack-time cakes and other baked goodies that we took for granted as children and now crave again as adults—what could be better with a cup of coffee than a slice of layer cake! For a fantastic finale to any family meal, look no further than Grandma's Delicious Desserts, which includes delicious pies, puddings, and crisps. For the ultimate in comfort food, nothing beats the delectably indulgent recipes in Grandma's Winter Warmers—hot, sugary treats, such as Apple Pie, taste all the better at the end of a chilly winter day. While Grandma's Special Treats are just that—enticing little cakes and cookies to enjoy at any time of day—you need no excuse to whip up a batch of grandma's delicious Chocolate Brownies or Caramel Shortbread.

Old meets new in this celebration of home-cooked treats that are perfect for sharing, and you can be sure that generations of grandmas have tried and tested every recipe—so each one is a piece of cake.

GRANDMA'S
FAMILY
FAVORITES

Raspberry Sponge Cake

SERVES 8–10
INGREDIENTS

- 1½ sticks salted butter, at room temperature, plus extra for greasing
- 2 cups superfine sugar or granulated sugar
- 3 eggs, beaten
- 1⅓ cups all-purpose flour
- 2 teaspoons baking powder
- pinch of salt
- 3 tablespoons raspberry preserves
- 1 tablespoon superfine sugar or confectioners' sugar, for dusting

1 Preheat the oven to 350°F.

2 Grease two 8-inch cake pans and line with parchment paper.

3 Cream together the butter and sugar in a mixing bowl, using a wooden spoon or an electric mixer, until the mixture is pale in color and light and fluffy.

4 Add the eggs a little at a time, beating well after each addition.

5 Sift together the flour, baking powder, and salt and carefully add to the mixture, folding in with a metal spoon or a spatula. Divide the batter between the pans and smooth over with the spatula.

6 Place the pans on the same shelf in the center of the preheated oven and bake for 25–30 minutes, until well risen, golden brown, and beginning to shrink from the sides of the pans.

7 Remove from the oven and let stand for 1 minute.

8 Loosen the cakes from around the edges of the pans using a spatula. Invert the cakes onto a clean dish towel, remove the paper, and invert them onto a wire rack (this avoids creating marks on the tops of the cakes from the wire rack).

9 When completely cool, sandwich together with the preserves and sprinkle with the sugar. The cake is delicious when freshly baked, but any remaining cake can be stored in an airtight container for up to one week.

Blueberry Crumb Cake

SERVES 12

INGREDIENTS

- 2 cups fresh blueberries
- 3⅔ cups all-purpose flour, plus extra for dusting
- 1½ tablespoons baking powder
- 1¼ teaspoons salt
- ½ teaspoon allspice
- 2¼ sticks salted butter, at room temperature, plus extra for greasing
- 1¾ cups superfine sugar or granulated sugar
- ½ teaspoon vanilla extract
- ½ teaspoon almond extract
- 2 extra-large eggs
- 1¼–1½ cups sour cream

CRUMB TOPPING

- 1 stick salted butter, diced
- 1 cup all-purpose flour
- 2 tablespoons packed light brown sugar
- 1 tablespoon granulated sugar
- 1 cup chopped almonds,

1 To make the crumb topping, put the butter and flour into a large bowl and rub together until the mixture resembles coarse bread crumbs. Stir in both types of sugar and the almonds, then let chill in the refrigerator until required.

2 Preheat the oven to 350°F. Grease a 13 x 9-inch rectangular cake pan and dust with flour. Dust the blueberries with 1 tablespoon of the measured flour and set aside. Sift the remaining flour into a bowl with the baking powder, salt, and allspice and set aside.

3 Place the butter in a large bowl and, using an electric mixer, beat until soft and creamy. Add the sugar, vanilla extract, and almond extract and continue beating until the mixture is light and fluffy. Add the eggs, one at a time, beating well after each addition, then beat in 1¼ cups of the sour cream. Beat in the flour until the mixture is soft and falls easily from a spoon. Add the remaining sour cream, 1 tablespoon at a time, if necessary.

4 Add the blueberries and any loose flour to the batter and quickly fold in. Pour the batter into the prepared pan and smooth the surface. Pinch the topping into large crumbs and spread evenly over the batter.

5 Bake the cake in the preheated oven for 45–55 minutes, until it comes away from the sides of the pan and a toothpick inserted into the center comes out clean. Transfer the pan to a wire rack and let cool completely. Cut the cake into twelve slices and serve straight from the pan.

Devil's Food Cake

SERVES 8–10

INGREDIENTS

- 5 ounces semisweet dark chocolate
- ½ cup whole milk
- 2 tablespoons unsweetened cocoa powder
- 1¼ sticks unsalted butter, plus extra for greasing
- ⅔ cup firmly packed light brown sugar
- 3 eggs, separated
- ¼ cup sour cream or crème fraîche
- 1⅔ cups all-purpose flour
- 1 teaspoon baking soda

FROSTING

- 5 ounces semisweet dark chocolate
- ½ cup unsweetened cocoa powder
- ¼ cup sour cream or crème fraîche
- 1 tablespoon light corn syrup
- 3 tablespoons unsalted butter
- ¼ cup water
- 1⅔ cups confectioners' sugar

1. Preheat the oven to 325°F. Grease two 8-inch cake pans and line the bottoms with parchment paper.

2. Break up the chocolate and place in a heatproof bowl over a saucepan of simmering water, add the milk and cocoa powder, then heat gently, stirring, until melted and smooth. Remove from the heat.

3. In a large bowl, beat together the butter and brown sugar until pale and fluffy. Add the egg yolks, then beat in the sour cream and the melted chocolate mixture.

4. Sift in the flour and baking soda, then fold in evenly. In a separate bowl, beat the egg whites until stiff enough to hold firm peaks. Fold into the batter lightly and evenly.

5. Divide the batter between the prepared cake pans, smooth level, and bake in the preheated oven for 35–40 minutes, or until risen and firm to the touch. Cool in the pans for 10 minutes, then invert onto a wire rack.

6. To make the frosting, put the chocolate, cocoa powder, sour cream, corn syrup, butter, and water in a saucepan and heat gently, until melted. Remove from the heat and sift in the sugar, stirring until smooth. Cool, stirring occasionally, until the mixture begins to thicken and hold its shape.

7. Slice the cakes in half horizontally with a sharp knife to make four layers. Sandwich together the cakes with about one-third of the frosting. Spread the remainder over the top and side of the cake, swirling with a spatula.

GRANDMA'S TIP

Use a metal, ceramic, or glass bowl when beating egg whites. Plastic bowls scratch easily, so may not be grease-free, which will prevent the whites from foaming.

Apple Streusel Cake

SERVES 8

INGREDIENTS

- 3 cooking apples (about 1 pound), such as Granny Smith
- 1⅓ cups all-purpose flour
- 2 teaspoons baking powder
- 1 teaspoon ground cinnamon
- pinch of salt
- 1 stick salted butter, plus extra for greasing
- ½ cup superfine sugar or granulated sugar
- 2 eggs
- 1–2 tablespoons whole milk
- confectioners' sugar, for dusting

STREUSEL TOPPING

- 1 cup all-purpose flour
- 1½ teaspoons baking powder
- 6 tablespoons salted butter
- ½ cup superfine sugar

1 Preheat the oven to 350°F. Grease a 9-inch springform cake pan. To make the streusel topping, sift the flour and baking powder into a bowl and rub in the butter until the mixture resembles coarse crumbs. Stir in the sugar and reserve.

2 To make the cake, peel, core, and thinly slice the apples. Sift the flour and baking powder into a bowl with the cinnamon and salt. Place the butter and sugar in a separate bowl and beat together until light and fluffy. Gradually beat in the eggs, adding a little of the flour mixture with the last addition of egg. Gently fold in half of the remaining flour mixture, then fold in the rest with the milk.

3 Spoon the batter into the prepared pan and smooth the top. Cover with the sliced apples and sprinkle the streusel topping evenly over the top.

4 Bake in the preheated oven for 1 hour, or until browned and firm to the touch. Let cool in the pan before opening the sides. Dust the cake with confectioners' sugar before serving.

Pineapple Upside-down Cake

SERVES 10

INGREDIENTS

- 4 eggs, beaten
- 1 cup superfine sugar or granulated sugar
- 1 teaspoon vanilla extract
- 1⅔ cups all-purpose flour
- 2 teaspoons baking powder
- 1 stick unsalted butter, melted, plus extra for greasing

TOPPING

- 3 tablespoons unsalted butter
- ¼ cup light corn syrup
- 1 (15½-ounce) can pineapple slices, drained
- 4–6 candied cherries, halved

1 Preheat the oven to 325°F. Grease a deep 9-inch round cake pan with a solid bottom and line the bottom with parchment paper.

2 To make the topping, place the butter and corn syrup in a heavy saucepan and heat gently until melted. Bring to a boil and boil for 2–3 minutes, stirring, until slightly thickened and toffee-like.

3 Pour the syrup into the bottom of the prepared pan. Arrange the pineapple slices and candied cherries in one layer over the syrup.

4 Place the eggs, sugar, and vanilla extract in a large heatproof bowl over a saucepan of gently simmering water and beat with an electric mixer for about 10–15 minutes, until thick enough to leave a trail when the beaters are lifted. Sift in the flour and baking powder and fold in lightly and evenly with a metal spoon.

5 Fold the melted butter into the batter with a metal spoon until evenly mixed. Spoon into the prepared pan and bake in the preheated oven for 1–1¼ hours, or until well risen, firm, and golden brown.

6 Let cool in the pan for 10 minutes, then carefully invert onto a serving plate. Serve warm or cold.

GRANDMA'S TIP

If your cake sinks in the middle, cut it out to make a ring cake, spread with whipped cream, and fill the center with fresh berries.

Angel Food Cake

SERVES 10

INGREDIENTS

- sunflower oil, for greasing
- 8 extra-large egg whites
- 1 teaspoon cream of tartar
- 1 teaspoon almond extract
- 1¼ cups superfine sugar or granulated sugar
- 1 cup all-purpose flour, plus extra for dusting

TO SERVE

- 2 cups mixed berries
- 1 tablespoon lemon juice
- 2 tablespoons confectioners' sugar

1 Preheat the oven to 325°F. Brush the inside of a 2-quart tube pan with oil and dust lightly with flour.

2 Beat the egg whites in a clean, grease-free bowl until they hold soft peaks. Add the cream of tartar and beat again until the whites are stiff but not dry.

3 Beat in the almond extract, then add the sugar, a tablespoon at a time, beating hard between each addition. Sift in the flour and fold in lightly and evenly, using a large metal spoon.

4 Spoon the batter into the prepared cake pan and tap on the work surface to remove any large air bubbles. Bake in the preheated oven for 40–45 minutes, or until golden brown and firm to the touch.

5 Run the tip of a small knife around the edges of the cake to loosen it from the pan. Let cool in the pan for 10 minutes, then invert onto a wire rack to finish cooling.

6 To serve, place the berries, lemon juice, and confectioners' sugar in a saucepan and heat gently until the sugar has dissolved. Serve with the cake.

Lemon Drizzle Cake

SERVES 8
INGREDIENTS

- butter, for greasing
- 1⅔ cups all-purpose flour
- 2 teaspoons baking powder
- 1 cup superfine sugar or granulated sugar
- 4 eggs
- ⅔ cup sour cream
- grated rind of 1 large lemon
- ¼ cup lemon juice
- ⅔ cup sunflower oil

SYRUP

- ¼ cup confectioners' sugar
- 3 tablespoons lemon juice

1 Preheat the oven to 350°F. Lightly grease an 8-inch, loose-bottom, round cake pan and line the bottom with parchment paper.

2 Sift together the flour and baking powder into a mixing bowl and stir in the sugar.

3 In a separate bowl, beat together the eggs, sour cream, lemon rind, lemon juice, and oil.

4 Pour the egg mixture into the dry ingredients and mix well until evenly combined.

5 Pour the batter into the prepared pan and bake in the preheated oven for 45–60 minutes, until risen and golden brown.

6 Meanwhile, to make the syrup, mix together the confectioners' sugar and lemon juice in a small saucepan. Stir over low heat until just beginning to bubble and turn syrupy.

7 As soon as the cake comes out of the oven, prick the surface with a toothpick, then brush the syrup over the top. Let the cake cool completely in the pan before inverting from the pan and serving.

Strawberry Shortcakes

SERVES 6
INGREDIENTS

- 1¾ cups all-purpose flour, plus extra for dusting
- 1 tablespoon baking powder
- ½ cup superfine sugar or granulated sugar
- 6 tablespoons unsalted butter, plus extra for greasing
- 1 egg, beaten
- 2–3 tablespoons whole milk, plus extra for brushing

FILLING

- 1 teaspoon vanilla extract
- 1 cup mascarpone cheese
- 3 tablespoons confectioners' sugar, plus extra for dusting
- 1 pint strawberries

1 Preheat the oven to 350°F. Lightly grease a large baking sheet.

2 Sift together the flour, baking powder, and sugar into a bowl. Rub in the butter with your fingertips until the mixture resembles bread crumbs. Beat the egg with 2 tablespoons of the milk and stir into the dry ingredients with a fork to form a soft, but not sticky, dough, adding more milk, if necessary.

3 Invert the dough onto a lightly floured surface and roll out to a thickness of about ¾ inch. Stamp out circles, using a 2¾-inch cookie cutter. Lightly press together the trimmings and stamp out more circles.

4 Place the circles on the prepared baking sheet and brush the tops lightly with milk. Bake in the preheated oven for 12–15 minutes, until firm and golden brown. Place on a wire rack to cool.

5 To make the filling, stir the vanilla extract into the mascarpone cheese with 2 tablespoons of the sugar. Reserve a few whole strawberries for decoration, then hull and slice the rest. Sprinkle with the remaining sugar.

6 Slice the shortcakes in half horizontally. Spoon half the mascarpone mixture onto the bottoms and top with the sliced strawberries. Spoon the remaining mascarpone mixture over the berries and replace the shortcake tops. To serve, dust the shortcakes with confectioners' sugar and top with the reserved whole strawberries.

GRANDMA'S
DELICIOUS
DESSERTS

Lemon Meringue Pie

SERVES 6–8
INGREDIENTS

PIE DOUGH
- 1¼ cups all-purpose flour, plus extra for dusting
- 6 tablespoons salted butter, cut into small pieces, plus extra for greasing
- ¼ cup confectioners' sugar, sifted
- finely grated rind of ½ lemon
- ½ egg yolk, beaten
- 1½ tablespoons whole milk

FILLING
- 3 tablespoons cornstarch
- 1¼ cups water
- juice and grated rind of 2 lemons
- 1 cup granulated sugar
- 2 eggs, separated

1 To make the dough, sift the flour into a bowl. Rub in the butter with your fingertips until the mixture resembles fine bread crumbs. Mix in the remaining ingredients. Invert onto a lightly floured work surface and knead briefly. Wrap in plastic wrap and chill in the refrigerator for 30 minutes.

2 Preheat the oven to 350°F. Grease an 8-inch round tart pan. Roll out the dough on a lightly floured work surface to a thickness of ¼ inch, then use it to line the bottom and sides of the pan. Prick all over with a fork, line with parchment paper and fill with pie weights or dried beans. Bake in the preheated oven for 15 minutes. Remove the pastry shell from the oven and take out the paper and weights. Reduce the oven temperature to 300°F.

3 To make the filling, mix the cornstarch with a little of the water to form a paste. Put the remaining water in a saucepan. Stir in the lemon juice, lemon rind, and cornstarch paste. Bring to the boil, stirring. Cook for 2 minutes. Let cool slightly. Stir in ⅓ cup of the granulated sugar and the egg yolks, then pour into the pastry shell.

4 Beat the egg whites in a clean, grease-free bowl until stiff. Gradually beat in the remaining granulated sugar and spread over the pie. Bake for 40 minutes. Remove from the oven, cool, and serve.

Banana Cream Pie

SERVES 8–10
INGREDIENTS

- flour, for dusting
- 1 store-bought rolled dough pie crust, thawed, if frozen
- 4 extra-large egg yolks
- ½ cup granulated sugar
- ¼ cup cornstarch
- pinch of salt
- 2 cups whole milk
- 1 teaspoon vanilla extract
- 3 bananas
- ½ tablespoon lemon juice
- 1½ cups heavy cream, whipped with ¼ cup confectioners' sugar, to serve

1 Preheat the oven to 400°F. Lightly flour a rolling pin and use to roll out the dough on a lightly floured work surface into a 12-inch circle. Line a 9-inch pie plate with the dough, then trim the excess dough and prick the bottom all over with a fork. Line the pastry shell with parchment paper and fill with pie weights or dried beans.

2 Bake in the preheated oven for 15 minutes, or until the pastry is a light golden color. Remove the paper and weights and prick the bottom again. Return to the oven and bake for an addtional 5–10 minutes, until golden and dry. Let cool completely on a wire rack.

3 Meanwhile, put the egg yolks, sugar, cornstarch, and salt into a bowl and beat until blended and pale. Beat in the milk and vanilla extract.

4 Pour the mixture into a heavy saucepan over medium–high heat and bring to a boil, stirring, until smooth and thick. Reduce the heat to low and simmer, stirring, for 2 minutes. Strain the mixture into a bowl and set aside to cool.

5 Slice the bananas, place in a bowl with the lemon juice, and toss. Arrange them in the cooled pastry shell, then top with the custard and chill in the refrigerator for at least 2 hours. Spread the cream over the top of the pie and serve immediately.

GRANDMA'S TIP
Old-fashioned metal pie plates, cake pans, and tart pans conduct heat better than glass, earthenware, or porcelain, producing even baking and reducing the cooking time.

Key Lime Pie

SERVES 8

INGREDIENTS

CRUMB CRUST
- 25 graham crackers or gingersnaps (about 6 ounces)
- 2 tablespoons granulated sugar
- ½ teaspoon ground cinnamon
- 5 tablespoons salted butter, melted, plus extra for greasing

FILLING
- 1 (14-ounce) can condensed milk
- ½ cup freshly squeezed lime juice
- finely grated rind of 3 limes
- 4 egg yolks
- whipped cream, to serve

1 Preheat the oven to 325°F. Lightly grease a 9-inch round tart pan, about 1½ inches deep.

2 To make the crumb crust, put the cookies, sugar, and cinnamon in a food processor and process until fine crumbs form—do not overprocess to a powder. Add the melted butter and process again until moistened.

3 Transfer the crumb mixture to the prepared tart pan and press over the bottom and up the sides. Place the tart pan on a baking sheet and bake in the preheated oven for 5 minutes.

4 Meanwhile, to make the filling, beat together the condensed milk, lime juice, lime rind, and egg yolks in a bowl until well blended.

5 Remove the tart pan from the oven, pour the filling into the crumb crust, and spread out to the edges. Return to the oven for an additional 15 minutes, or until the filling is set around the edges but still wobbly in the center.

6 Let cool completely on a wire rack, then cover and chill for at least 2 hours. Spread thickly with whipped cream and serve.

Rhubarb Crisp

SERVES 6
INGREDIENTS

- 2 pounds rhubarb
- ½ cup granulated sugar
- grated rind and juice of 1 orange
- Homemade Vanilla Custard (see page 60), to serve

CRUMB TOPPING
- 1¾ cups all-purpose flour or whole-wheat flour
- 1 stick salted butter
- ½ cup firmly packed light brown sugar
- 1 teaspoon ground ginger

1 Preheat the oven to 375°F.

2 Cut the rhubarb into 1-inch lengths and place in a 2-quart ovenproof dish with the sugar and the orange rind and juice.

3 To make the crumb topping, place the flour in a mixing bowl and rub in the butter until the mixture resembles coarse crumbs. Stir in the sugar and the ginger.

4 Spread the topping evenly over the fruit and press down lightly using a fork.

5 Place on a baking sheet and bake in the center of the preheated oven for 25–30 minutes, until the topping is golden brown. Serve warm with custard.

GRANDMA'S TIP
Use young shoots of rhubarb because they are the sweetest. A handful of strawberries make a good addition because they will enhance the flavor and color.

New York Cheesecake

SERVES 10
INGREDIENTS

- 1 stick salted butter, plus extra for greasing
- 1¼ cups finely crushed graham crackers
- 1¼ cups granulated sugar
- 4 cups cream cheese
- 2 tablespoons all-purpose flour
- 1 teaspoon vanilla extract
- finely grated zest of 1 orange
- finely grated zest of 1 lemon
- 3 eggs
- 2 egg yolks
- 1¼ cups heavy cream

1 Preheat the oven to 350°F. Place a small saucepan over low heat, add the butter, and heat until it melts. Remove from the heat, stir in the crushed graham crackers and 1 tablespoon of the granulated sugar, and mix through.

2 Press the crumb mixture tightly into the bottom of a 9-inch springform cake pan. Place in the preheated oven and bake for 10 minutes. Remove from the oven and let cool on a wire rack.

3 Increase the oven temperature to 400°F. Using an electric mixer, beat the cheese until creamy, then gradually add the remaining granulated sugar and flour and beat until smooth. Increase the speed and beat in the vanilla extract, orange zest, and lemon zest, then beat in the eggs and egg yolks one at a time. Finally, beat in the cream. Scrape any excess from the beaters of the mixer into the batter.

4 Grease the sides of the cake pan and pour in the batter. Smooth the top, transfer to the oven, and bake for 15 minutes, then reduce the temperature to 225°F and bake for an additional 30 minutes. Turn off the oven and let the cheesecake stand in it for 2 hours to cool and set. Cover and chill in the refrigerator overnight.

5 Slide a knife around the edge of the cake then unfasten the pan, cut the cheesecake into slices, and serve.

Chocolate Pudding

SERVES 4–6
INGREDIENTS

- ½ cup granulated sugar
- ¼ cup unsweetened cocoa powder
- 2 tablespoons cornstarch
- pinch of salt
- 1½ cups whole milk
- 1 egg, beaten
- 4 tablespoons unsalted butter
- ½ teaspoon vanilla extract
- heavy cream, to serve

1 Put the sugar, cocoa powder, cornstarch, and salt into a heatproof bowl, stir, and set aside.

2 Pour the milk into a saucepan and heat over medium heat until just simmering. Do not bring to a boil.

3 Keeping the pan over medium heat, spoon a little of the simmering milk into the sugar mixture and blend, then stir this mixture into the milk in the pan. Beat in the egg and half the butter and reduce the heat to low.

4 Simmer for 5–8 minutes, stirring frequently, until the mixture thickens. Remove from the heat and add the vanilla extract and the remaining butter, stirring until the butter melts and is absorbed.

5 The pudding can be served hot or chilled, with cream for pouring over. If chilling the pudding, spoon it into a serving bowl and let cool completely, then press plastic wrap onto the surface to prevent a skin from forming and chill in the refrigerator until required.

Apple Fritters

MAKES 12 FRITTERS
INGREDIENTS

- 2 cooking apples, such as Granny Smith, peeled, cored, and diced
- 1 teaspoon lemon juice
- 2 eggs, separated
- sunflower oil, for deep-frying and greasing
- ⅔ cup whole milk
- 1 tablespoon salted butter, melted
- ½ cup all-purpose white flour
- ½ cup whole-wheat flour
- 2 tablespoons sugar
- ¼ teaspoon salt

CINNAMON GLAZE
- ½ cup confectioners' sugar
- ½ teaspoon ground cinnamon
- 1 tablespoon whole milk, plus extra, if needed

1 To make the cinnamon glaze, sift the sugar and cinnamon into a small bowl and make a well in the center. Slowly stir in the milk until smooth, then set aside.

2 Put the apples in a small bowl, add the lemon juice, toss, and set aside. Beat the egg whites in a separate bowl until stiff peaks form, then set aside.

3 Heat enough oil for deep-frying in a deep-fat fryer or heavy saucepan until it reaches 350°F, or until a cube of bread browns in 30 seconds.

4 Meanwhile, put the egg yolks and milk into a large bowl and beat together, then stir in the butter. Sift in the white flour, whole-wheat flour, sugar, and salt, adding any bran left in the sifter, then stir the dry ingredients into the wet ingredients until just combined. Stir in the apples and their juices, then fold in the egg whites.

5 Lightly grease a spoon and use it to drop batter into the hot oil, without overcrowding the pan. Fry the fritters for 2–3 minutes, turning once, until golden brown on both sides. Transfer to paper towels to drain, then transfer to a wire rack. Repeat until all the batter is used.

6 Stir the glaze and add a little extra milk, if necessary, so that it flows freely from the tip of a spoon. Drizzle the glaze over the fritters and let stand for 3–5 minutes until firm. Serve immediately.

GRANDMA'S TIP
If not serving the fritters right away, sift some confectioners' sugar, cinnamon, and a pinch of nutmeg over them, then let cool.

Pecan Pie

SERVES 8
INGREDIENTS

PIE DOUGH

- 1⅔ cups all-purpose flour, plus extra for dusting
- 1 stick unsalted butter
- 2 tablespoons granulated sugar
- 2–3 tablespoons cold water

FILLING

- 5 tablespoons unsalted butter
- ½ cup firmly packed light brown sugar
- ½ cup light corn syrup
- 2 extra-large eggs, beaten
- 1 teaspoon vanilla extract
- 1 cup pecans

1 To make the dough, place the flour in a bowl and rub in the butter with your fingertips until it resembles fine bread crumbs. Stir in the sugar and add enough cold water to mix to a firm dough. Wrap in plastic wrap and chill for 15 minutes, until firm enough to roll out.

2 Preheat the oven to 400°F. Roll out the dough on a lightly floured work surface and use to line a 9-inch loose-bottom round tart pan. Prick the bottom with a fork and chill for 15 minutes.

3 Place the tart pan on a baking sheet, line with a sheet of parchment paper and fill with pie weights or dried beans. Bake in the preheated oven for 10 minutes. Remove the weights and paper and bake for an additional 5 minutes. Reduce the oven temperature to 350°F.

4 To make the filling, place the butter, sugar, and corn syrup in a saucepan and heat gently until melted. Remove from the heat and quickly beat in the eggs and vanilla extract.

5 Coarsely chop the nuts and stir into the mixture. Pour into the pastry shell and bake for 35–40 minutes, until the filling is just set. Serve warm or cold.

GRANDMA'S TIP
Add 2 tablespoons of dark rum to the filling just before removing it from the heat. This will balance the sweetness and bring out the rich flavors.

GRANDMA'S WINTER WARMERS

Bread & Butter Pudding

SERVES 4–6
INGREDIENTS

- 6 tablespoons salted butter, softened
- 6 slices of thick white bread
- ⅓ cup mixed dried fruit, such as golden raisins, dried currants, and raisins
- 2 tablespoons candied peel
- 3 extra-large eggs
- 1¼ cups whole milk
- ⅔ cup heavy cream
- ¼ cup granulated sugar
- whole nutmeg, for grating
- 1 tablespoon demerara sugar
- light cream, to serve (optional)

1 Preheat the oven to 350°F. Use a little of the butter to grease an 8 x 10-inch ovenproof dish. Butter the slices of bread, cut them into quarters, and arrange half of the slices overlapping in the prepared ovenproof dish.

2 Sprinkle half the fruit and candied peel over the bread, cover with the remaining bread slices, then add the remaining fruit and candied peel.

3 In a small bowl, beat the eggs well and mix in the milk, cream, and sugar. Pour over the bread slices and let stand for 15 minutes to allow the bread to soak up some of the egg mixture. Tuck the fruit under the uppermost layer of bread, to prevent it from burning.

4 Grate nutmeg to taste over the top of the pudding, then sprinkle with the demerara sugar.

5 Place the pudding on a baking sheet and bake at the top of the preheated oven for 30–40 minutes, until just set and golden brown.

6 Remove from the oven and serve warm with a little cream, if using.

GRANDMA'S TIP
Try using brioche or slices of raisin bread instead of white bread. Any mixture of dried fruits can be used. Why not experiment with your favorites?

Baked Rice Pudding

SERVES 4–6

INGREDIENTS

- 1 tablespoon melted unsalted butter
- ½ cup short-grain rice
- ¼ cup granulated sugar
- 3½ cups whole milk
- ½ teaspoon vanilla extract
- 3 tablespoons unsalted butter, chilled
- whole nutmeg, for grating
- light cream, to serve (optional)

1 Preheat the oven to 300°F. Grease a 5-cup/1-quart ovenproof dish (a gratin dish is good) with the melted butter, place the rice in the dish, and sprinkle with the sugar.

2 Heat the milk in a saucepan until almost boiling, then pour over the rice. Add the vanilla extract and stir well to dissolve the sugar.

3 Cut the butter into small pieces and place them over the surface of the pudding.

4 Grate nutmeg to taste over the top. Place the dish on a baking sheet and bake in the center of the preheated oven for 1½–2 hours, until the pudding is browned on the top. Stir after the first 30 minutes of cooking to disperse the rice. Serve hot, topped with cream, if using.

GRANDMA'S TIP

When measuring honey or syrup, dip the measuring spoon in hot water and dry it first to prevent them from sticking.

Baked Spicy Pudding

SERVES 4–6

INGREDIENTS

- 2 tablespoons raisins or golden raisins
- ⅓ cup cornmeal
- 1½ cups whole milk
- ¼ cup molasses
- 2 tablespoons packed dark brown sugar
- ¼ teaspoon salt
- 2 tablespoons butter, diced, plus extra for greasing
- 2 teaspoons ground ginger
- ¼ teaspoon cinnamon
- ¼ teaspoon ground nutmeg
- 2 eggs, beaten
- vanilla ice cream, to serve

1 Preheat the oven to 300°F. Grease a 5-cup/1-quart ovenproof dish and set aside. Put the raisins in a strainer with 1 tablespoon of the cornmeal and toss well together. Shake off the excess cornmeal and set aside.

2 Put the milk and molasses into a saucepan over medium–high heat and stir until the molasses is dissolved. Add the sugar and salt and continue stirring until the sugar is dissolved. Sprinkle with the remaining cornmeal and bring to a boil, stirring continuously. Reduce the heat and simmer for 3–5 minutes, until the mixture is thickened.

3 Remove the pan from the heat, add the butter, ginger, cinnamon, and nutmeg, and stir until the butter is melted. Add the eggs and beat until they are incorporated, then stir in the raisins. Pour the mixture into the prepared dish.

4 Put the dish in a small roasting pan and pour in enough boiling water to come halfway up the side of the dish. Put the dish in the preheated oven and bake, uncovered, for 1¾–2 hours, until the pudding is set and a toothpick inserted in the center comes out clean.

5 Serve immediately, straight from the dish, with a scoopful of ice cream on top.

Pumpkin Pie

SERVES 6

INGREDIENTS

- 1 cup all-purpose flour, plus extra for dusting
- ¼ teaspoon baking powder
- 1½ teaspoons ground cinnamon
- ¾ teaspoon ground nutmeg
- ¾ teaspoon ground cloves
- 1 teaspoon salt
- ¼ cup granulated sugar
- 4 tablespoons cold unsalted butter, diced, plus extra for greasing
- 3 eggs
- 1 (15-ounce) can pumpkin puree
- 1 (14-ounce) can condensed milk
- ½ teaspoon vanilla extract
- 1 tablespoon demerara sugar or other raw sugar

TOPPING

- 2 tablespoons all-purpose flour
- ¼ cup demerara sugar or other raw sugar
- 1 teaspoon ground cinnamon
- 2 tablespoons cold unsalted butter, diced
- ¾ cup chopped pecans
- ⅔ cup chopped walnuts

1 Grease a 9-inch round tart pan. Sift the flour and baking powder into a large bowl. Stir in ½ teaspoon of the cinnamon, ¼ teaspoon of the nutmeg, ¼ teaspoon of the cloves, ½ teaspoon of the salt, and all the granulated sugar.

2 Rub in the butter with your fingertips until the mixture resembles fine bread crumbs, then make a well in the center. Lightly beat one of the eggs and pour it into the well. Mix together with a wooden spoon, then shape the dough into a ball.

3 Invert the dough onto a lightly floured work surface, roll out, and use to line the prepared pan. Trim the edges, then cover and chill for 30 minutes.

4 Preheat the oven to 425°F. Put the pumpkin puree in a large bowl, then stir in the condensed milk and the remaining eggs. Add the remaining spices and salt, then stir in the vanilla extract and demerara sugar. Pour into the pastry shell and bake in the preheated oven for 15 minutes.

5 Meanwhile, make the topping. Mix together the flour, sugar, and cinnamon in a bowl, rub in the butter, then stir in the nuts. Remove the pie from the oven and reduce the oven temperature to 350°F. Sprinkle the topping over the pie, then return to the oven and bake for an additional 35 minutes.

Apple Turnovers

MAKES 8 TURNOVERS
INGREDIENTS

- 1 sheet ready-to-bake puff pastry, thawed, if frozen
- whole milk, for glazing

FILLING
- 3 cooking apples (about 1 pound), such as Granny Smith peeled, cored, and chopped
- grated rind of 1 lemon (optional)
- pinch of ground cloves (optional)
- 3 tablespoons granulated sugar

ORANGE SUGAR
- 1 tablespoon granulated sugar, for sprinkling
- finely grated rind of 1 orange

ORANGE CREAM
- 1 cup heavy cream
- grated rind of 1 orange and juice of ½ orange
- confectioners' sugar, to taste

1 Prepare the filling before rolling out the pastry. Mix together the apples, lemon rind, and ground cloves, if using, but do not add the sugar until the last minute, because it will cause the juice to seep out of the apples. For the orange sugar, mix together the sugar and orange rind.

2 Preheat the oven to 425°F. Roll out the pastry on a floured work surface into a 24 x 12-inch rectangle. Cut the pastry in half lengthwise, then across into four to make eight 6-inch squares. You can do this in two batches, rolling half of the pastry out into a 12-inch square and cutting it into quarters, if preferred.

3 Mix the sugar into the apple filling. Brush each square lightly with milk and place a little of the apple filling in the center. Fold over one corner diagonally to meet the opposite one, making a triangular turnover, and press the edges together firmly. Place on a nonstick baking sheet. Repeat with the remaining squares.

4 Brush the turnovers with milk and sprinkle with a little of the orange sugar. Bake for 15–20 minutes, until puffed and well browned. Cool the turnovers on a wire rack.

5 For the orange cream, whip together the cream, orange rind, and orange juice until thick. Add a little sugar to taste and whip again until the cream just holds soft peaks. Serve the turnovers warm, with spoonfuls of orange cream.

GRANDMA'S TIP
For something extra warming, try adding some cinnamon, or replace the lemon rind with orange rind and a teaspoon of marmalade.

Apple Pie

SERVES 6
INGREDIENTS

PIE DOUGH
- 2¾ cups all-purpose flour
- pinch of salt
- 6 tablespoons salted butter or margarine, cut into small pieces
- ⅓ cup lard or vegetable shortening, cut into small pieces
- about ⅓ cup cold water
- beaten egg or whole milk, for glazing

FILLING
- 6 cooking apples (about 2 pounds), such as Granny Smith, peeled, cored, and sliced
- ½ cup firmly packed light brown sugar or granulated sugar, plus extra for sprinkling
- ½–1 teaspoon ground cinnamon, allspice, or ground ginger
- 1–2 tablespoons water (optional)

1 To make the pie dough, sift the flour and salt into a mixing bowl. Add the butter and lard and rub in with your fingertips until the mixture resembles fine bread crumbs. Add the water and gather the mixture together into a dough. Wrap the dough in plastic wrap and chill in the refrigerator for 30 minutes.

2 Preheat the oven to 425°F. Roll out almost two-thirds of the dough thinly and use to line a deep 9-inch pie plate or pie pan.

3 To make the filling, mix the apples with the sugar and spice and pack into the pastry shell. Add the water if needed, particularly if the apples are not juicy.

4 Roll out the remaining dough to form a lid. Dampen the edges of the pie rim with water and position the lid, pressing the edges firmly together. Trim and crimp the edges.

5 Using the trimmings, cut out leaves or other shapes to decorate the top of the pie. Dampen and attach. Glaze the top of the pie with the beaten egg and make one or two slits in the top.

6 Place the pie on a baking sheet and bake in the preheated oven for 20 minutes, then reduce the oven temperature to 350°F and bake for an additional 30 minutes, or until the pastry is a light golden brown. Serve hot or cold, sprinkled with sugar.

GRANDMA'S TIP
Prevent apples from discoloring by placing the peeled slices in a bowl of water with the juice of 1 lemon added.

Date Cake with Caramel Sauce

SERVES 4

INGREDIENTS

- ½ cup golden raisins
- 1 cup chopped, pitted dates
- 1 teaspoon baking soda
- 2 tablespoons salted butter, plus extra for greasing
- 1 cup firmly packed light brown sugar
- 2 eggs
- 1⅔ cups all-purpose flour
- 2½ teaspoons baking powder

CARAMEL SAUCE

- 2 tablespoons salted butter
- ¾ cup heavy cream
- 1 cup firmly packed light brown sugar
- zested rind of 1 orange, to decorate

1 To make the cake, put the golden raisins, dates, and baking soda into a heatproof bowl. Cover with boiling water and let soak.

2 Preheat the oven to 350°F. Grease a round cake pan, 8 inches in diameter.

3 Put the butter in a separate bowl, add the sugar, and mix well. Beat in the eggs, then sift the flour and baking powder over the mixture and fold in. Drain the soaked fruit, add to the bowl, and mix. Spoon the batter evenly into the prepared cake pan.

4 Transfer to the preheated oven and bake for 35–40 minutes. The cake is cooked when a toothpick inserted into the center comes out clean.

5 About 5 minutes before the end of the cooking time, make the sauce. Melt the butter in a saucepan over medium heat. Stir in the cream and sugar and bring to a boil, stirring continuously. Reduce the heat and simmer for 5 minutes.

6 Invert the cake onto a serving plate and pour the sauce over it. Decorate with zested orange rind and serve.

GRANDMA'S TIP

You can make this wicked dessert in individual molds so that everyone has their own serving. Cook for 20–25 minutes and then invert onto serving plates.

Homemade Vanilla Custard

SERVES 4–6
INGREDIENTS

- 1¼ cups whole milk
- 2 eggs
- 2 teaspoons superfine sugar or granulated sugar
- 1 vanilla bean, split, or 1 teaspoon vanilla extract

1 Put 2 tablespoons of the milk, the eggs, and sugar into a heatproof bowl that will fit over a saucepan of simmering water without the bottom of the bowl touching the water, then set aside.

2 Put the remaining milk into a small, heavy saucepan over medium–high heat and heat just until small bubbles appear around the edge. Scrape half the vanilla seeds into the milk and add the bean. Remove the pan from the heat, cover, and let steep for 30 minutes.

3 Bring a few inches of water to a boil in the saucepan chosen for the heatproof bowl, then reduce the heat to low.

4 Meanwhile, using an electric mixer, beat the milk, eggs, and sugar in the heatproof bowl until pale and thick. Slowly beat in the warm milk. Place over the pan of simmering water and cook, stirring continuously, for 10–15 minutes, until the sauce becomes thick enough to hold the impression of your finger if you rub it along the back of the spoon. It is important that the bottom of the bowl never touches the water and that the sauce doesn't boil. If the sauce looks as if it is about to boil, remove the bowl from the pan and continue stirring.

5 Strain the hot custard into a separate bowl. If you have not used a vanilla bean and seeds, stir in the vanilla extract. The custard can be used immediately, or let it cool completely, then cover and chill for up to one day. The sauce will thicken on cooling.

GRANDMA'S TIP
Keep the used vanilla bean in a jar of sugar and use the flavored sugar for making cakes, sprinkling over fruit, or making dessert sauces.

GRANDMA'S SPECIAL TREATS

Chocolate Brownies

MAKES 16 BROWNIES
INGREDIENTS

- peanut oil, for greasing
- 8 ounces good-quality semisweet chocolate, at least 60 percent cocoa solids
- 1½ sticks salted butter
- 3 extra-large eggs
- ½ cup granulated sugar
- 1⅓ cups all-purpose flour
- 2 teaspoons baking powder
- 1 cup walnuts or blanched hazelnuts, chopped
- ¼ cup milk chocolate chips

1 Preheat the oven to 350°F. Lightly grease a shallow 10-inch square nonstick baking pan.

2 Break the chocolate into a heatproof bowl and place over a small saucepan of simmering water. It is important that the bottom of the bowl doesn't touch the water.

3 Add the butter to the chocolate, set the bowl over the saucepan, and heat the water to a slow simmer. Heat the chocolate and leave undisturbed to melt slowly—this will take about 10 minutes. Remove the bowl from the pan and stir well to combine the chocolate and the butter.

4 Meanwhile, beat together the eggs and sugar in a bowl until pale cream in color. Stir in the melted chocolate mixture, then add the flour, baking powder, nuts and chocolate chips. Mix everything together well.

5 Transfer the batter to the prepared baking pan and bake in the preheated oven for 30 minutes, or until the top is set—the center should still be slightly sticky. Let cool in the pan, then lift out and cut into squares.

Classic Oatmeal Cookies

MAKES 30 COOKIES

INGREDIENTS

- 1½ sticks salted butter, plus extra for greasing
- 1⅓ cups packed light brown sugar
- 1 egg
- ½ cup water
- 1 teaspoon vanilla extract
- 4 cups rolled oats
- 1 cup all-purpose flour
- 1 teaspoon salt
- ½ teaspoon baking soda

1 Preheat the oven to 350°F and grease a large baking sheet.

2 Cream together the butter and sugar in a large mixing bowl. Beat in the egg, water, and vanilla extract until the mixture is smooth. In a separate bowl, mix together the oats, flour, salt, and baking soda.

3 Gradually stir the oat mixture into the butter mixture until thoroughly combined.

4 Place tablespoonfuls of the dough onto the prepared baking sheet, making sure they are well spaced. Transfer to the preheated oven and bake for 15 minutes, or until golden brown.

5 Using a spatula, carefully transfer the cookies to wire racks to cool completely.

Mega Chip Cookies

MAKES 12 LARGE COOKIES

INGREDIENTS

- 2 sticks butter, softened
- ¾ cup granulated sugar
- 1 egg yolk, lightly beaten
- 2 teaspoons vanilla extract
- 1¾ cups all-purpose flour
- ⅔ cup unsweetened cocoa powder
- pinch of salt
- ½ cup milk chocolate chips
- ½ cup white chocolate chips
- 4 ounces semisweet dark chocolate, coarsely chopped

1 Preheat the oven to 375°F. Line 2–3 baking sheets with parchment paper.

2 Put the butter and sugar into a bowl and mix well with a wooden spoon, then beat in the egg yolk and vanilla extract. Sift together the flour, cocoa powder, and salt into the mixture, then add the milk chocolate chips and white chocolate chips and stir until thoroughly combined.

3 Make 12 balls of the mixture, place them on the prepared baking sheets, spaced well apart, and flatten slightly. Press the pieces of dark chocolate into the cookies.

4 Bake in the preheated oven for 12–15 minutes. Let cool on the baking sheets for 5–10 minutes, then, using a spatula, carefully transfer the cookies to wire racks to cool completely.

Raisin Bran Muffins

MAKES 12 MUFFINS
INGREDIENTS

- 1 cup all-purpose flour
- 1 tablespoon baking powder
- 2½ cups wheat bran
- ½ cup granulated sugar
- 1 cup raisins
- 2 eggs
- 2 cups skim milk
- ⅓ cup sunflower oil, plus extra for greasing
- 1 teaspoon vanilla extract

1 Preheat the oven to 400°F. Grease a 12-cup muffin pan or line with 12 muffin cups. Sift together the flour and baking powder into a large bowl. Stir in the bran, sugar, and raisins.

2 Lightly beat the eggs in a bowl, then beat in the milk, oil, and vanilla extract. Make a well in the center of the dry ingredients and pour in the beaten liquid ingredients. Stir gently until just combined; do not overmix.

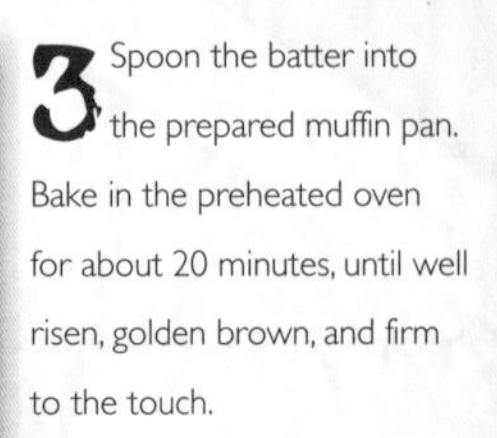

3 Spoon the batter into the prepared muffin pan. Bake in the preheated oven for about 20 minutes, until well risen, golden brown, and firm to the touch.

4 Let the muffins cool in the pan for 5 minutes, then serve warm or transfer to a wire rack to cool completely.

Cinnamon Swirls

MAKES 12 SWIRLS
INGREDIENTS

- 1⅔ cups white bread flour
- ½ teaspoon salt
- 2¼ teaspoons active dry yeast
- 2 tablespoons salted butter, cut into small pieces, plus extra for greasing
- 1 egg, lightly beaten
- ½ cup lukewarm whole milk
- 2 tablespoons maple syrup, for glazing

FILLING
- 4 tablespoons salted butter, softened
- 2 teaspoons ground cinnamon
- ¼ cup firmly packed light brown sugar
- ⅓ cup dried currants

1 Grease a baking sheet with a little butter.

2 Sift the flour and salt into a mixing bowl. Stir in the yeast. Rub in the butter with your fingertips until the mixture resembles bread crumbs. Add the egg and milk and mix to form a dough.

3 Form the dough into a ball, place in a greased bowl, cover, and let stand in a warm place for about 40 minutes, or until doubled in size.

4 Lightly knead the dough for 1 minute, then roll out to a rectangle measuring 12 x 9 inches.

5 To make the filling, cream together the butter, cinnamon, and sugar until light and fluffy. Spread the filling evenly over the dough rectangle, leaving a 1-inch border all around. Sprinkle the currants evenly over the top.

6 Roll up the dough from one of the long edges, and press down to seal. Cut the roll into 12 slices. Place them, cut side down, on the baking sheet, cover, and let stand for 30 minutes.

7 Meanwhile, preheat the oven to 375°F. Bake the swirls in the preheated oven for 20–30 minutes, or until well risen. Brush with the maple syrup and let cool slightly before serving.

Chocolate Fudge

MAKES 32 PIECES
INGREDIENTS

- 2 tablespoons unsweetened cocoa powder
- 1¼ cups whole milk
- 5 ounces semisweet dark chocolate, at least 85 percent cocoa solids, finely chopped
- 4 cups superfine sugar or granulated sugar
- 1 stick salted butter, chopped, plus extra for greasing
- pinch of salt
- 1½ teaspoons vanilla extract
- 1½ cups pecans, walnuts, or toasted hazelnuts, or a mixture of nuts, chopped

1 Put the cocoa powder into a small bowl, add 2 tablespoons of the milk, and stir until blended. Pour the remaining milk into a large, heavy saucepan, then add the cocoa mixture and chocolate and simmer over medium–high heat, stirring, until the chocolate melts. Add the sugar, butter, and salt, reduce the heat to low, and stir until the butter is melted, the sugar is dissolved, and you can't feel any of the grains when you rub a spoon against the side of the pan.

2 Increase the heat and bring the mixture to a boil. Cover the pan and boil for 2 minutes, then uncover and carefully clip a candy thermometer to the side. Continue boiling, without stirring, until the temperature reaches 247°F, or until a small amount of the mixture forms a soft ball when dropped in cold water.

3 Meanwhile, line an 8-inch square cake pan with aluminum foil, grease the foil, then set aside.

4 Remove the pan from the heat, stir in the vanilla extract, and beat the fudge until it thickens. Stir in the nuts.

5 Pour the fudge mixture into the prepared pan and use a wet spatula to smooth the surface. Set aside and let stand for at least 2 hours to become firm. Lift the fudge out of the pan, then peel off the foil. Cut the fudge into eight 1-inch strips, then cut each strip into four pieces. Store the fudge for up to one week in an airtight container.

Caramel Shortbread

MAKES 12 SLICES
INGREDIENTS

- 1 stick salted butter, plus extra for greasing
- 1⅓ cups all-purpose flour
- ¼ cup granulated sugar
- 7 ounces semisweet dark chocolate, broken into pieces

FILLING
- 1½ sticks salted butter
- ½ cup granulated sugar
- 3 tablespoons light corn syrup
- 1 (14-ounce) can condensed milk

1 Preheat the oven to 350°F. Grease and line the bottom of a shallow 9-inch square cake pan.

2 Place the butter, flour, and sugar in a food processor and process until the mixture begins to bind together. Press it into the prepared pan and smooth the top. Bake in the preheated oven for 20–25 minutes, or until golden.

3 Meanwhile, make the filling. Place the butter, sugar, corn syrup, and condensed milk in a saucepan and heat gently over low heat until the sugar is dissolved.

4 Bring to a boil and simmer for 6–8 minutes, stirring continuously, until the mixture becomes thick. Pour caramel over the shortbread and chill in the refrigerator until firm.

5 Place the chocolate in a heatproof bowl set over a saucepan of gently simmering water and stir until melted. Let cool slightly, then spread over the caramel. Chill in the refrigerator until set. Cut the shortbread into 12 pieces with a sharp knife and serve.

GRANDMA'S TIP
Caramel Shortbread, also known as Caramel Slices or Millionaires' Shortbread, is thought to be of Scottish origin.

Icebox Cookies

MAKES 50–60 COOKIES
INGREDIENTS

- 2⅔ cups all-purpose flour
- 2 tablespoons unsweetened cocoa powder
- ½ teaspoon baking soda
- 1 teaspoon ground ginger
- ½ teaspoon ground cinnamon
- ½ cup molasses
- ¼ cup boiling water
- 1 stick butter, softened
- ¼ cup granulated sugar
- confectioners' sugar, for dusting

1 Sift together the flour, cocoa powder, baking soda, ginger, and cinnamon into a bowl, then set aside. Mix the molasses with the water and set aside.

2 Put the butter into a large bowl and beat with an electric mixer until creamy. Slowly add the granulated sugar and continue beating until light and fluffy. Gradually add the flour mixture, alternating it with the molasses mixture to form a soft dough.

3 Scrape equal amounts of the dough onto two pieces of plastic wrap and roll into logs, using the wrap as a guide, each about 7½ inches long and 1½ inches thick. Put the dough logs in the refrigerator for 2 hours, then transfer to the freezer for at least 2 hours and up to 2 months.

4 When ready to bake, preheat the oven to 350°F and line two or three baking sheets, depending on how many cookies you are baking, with parchment paper. Unwrap the dough logs, trim the ends, and cut into ¼-inch slices. Rewrap any unused dough and return to the freezer.

5 Place the dough slices on the prepared baking sheets and bake in the preheated oven for 12 minutes. Remove from the oven, let cool on the baking sheets for 3 minutes, then transfer to wire racks, dust with confectioners' sugar and let cool completely.

Butterfly Cupcakes

MAKES 12 CUPCAKES
INGREDIENTS

- 1 cup all-purpose flour
- 2 teaspoons baking powder
- 1 stick salted butter, softened
- ½ cup granulated sugar
- 2 eggs, beaten
- finely grated rind of ½ lemon
- 2–4 tablespoons whole milk
- confectioners' sugar, sifted, for dusting

FILLING
- 4 tablespoons salted butter
- 1 cup confectioners' sugar
- 1 tablespoon lemon juice

1 Preheat the oven to 375°F. Place 12 cupcake liners in a muffin pan. Sift together the flour and baking powder into a bowl. Add the butter, sugar, eggs, lemon rind, and enough milk to form a medium-soft consistency.

2 Beat the batter thoroughly until smooth, then divide among the cupcake liners and bake in the preheated oven for 15–20 minutes, or until well risen and golden. Transfer to wire racks to cool.

3 To make the filling, place the butter in a bowl. Sift in the confectioners' sugar and add the lemon juice. Beat well until smooth and creamy. When the cakes are completely cooled, use a serrated knife to cut a circle from the top of each cake, then cut each circle in half.

4 Spoon a little filling into the center of each cake and press the two semicircular pieces into it to resemble wings. Dust the cakes with confectioners' sugar before serving.

GRANDMA'S TIP
Cupcakes are always a favorite with children. You can use multicolored or patterned cupcake liners to make these look even cuter.

Index